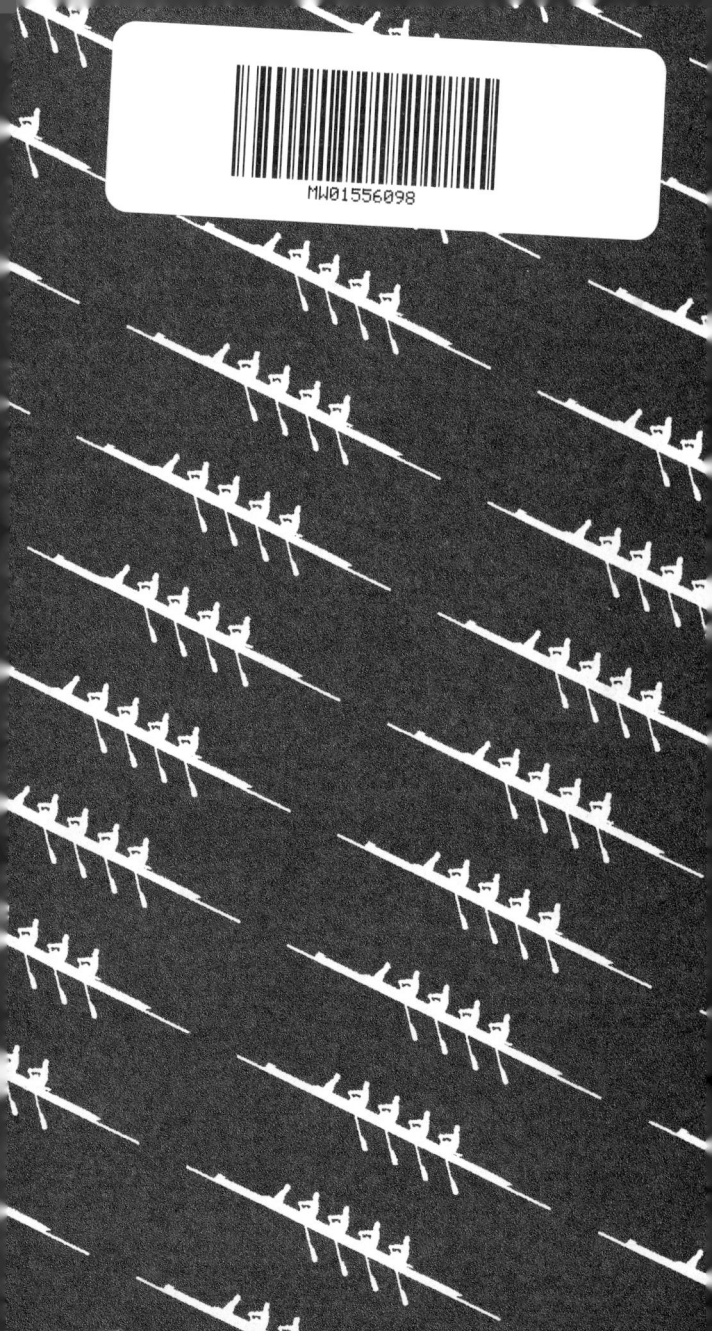

Teamwork
Quote/Unquote

APPLEWOOD BOOKS
BEDFORD, MASSACHUSETTS

Copyright © 2002 Applewood Books, Inc.

Quotations Copyright © 2002 U-inspire, Inc.

*T*hank you for purchasing an Applewood Book. Applewood reprints America's lively classics—books from the past that are still of interest to modern readers. For a free copy of our current catalog, please write to Applewood Books, P.O. Box 365, Bedford, MA 01730

ISBN 1-55709-977-4

Library of Congress Control Number: 2001092159

10 9 8 7 6 5 4 3 2 1

Introduction

Whoever you are and whatever you do, you are probably a part of many teams. Whether it be on the job, on the field, in the community or at home, one thing is certain . . . you succeed when your team succeeds.

The question we asked ourselves when creating this compilation is "What makes a great team?" One quality (which can be found in the "Quote" side of this collection) is that a great team consists of people who work well together. Another quality (which can be found in the "Unquote" side of this collection) is that a great team is made up of strong individual performers.

While we think that a great team incorporates both of these characteristics, we will leave it up to you to draw your own conclusions. Most of all, we hope that you enjoy this collection and find the wisdom and motivation to make your teams better!

Quote

Quote

Build for your team a feeling of oneness, of dependence on one another and of strength to be derived by unity.
—Vince Lombardi

Few things can help an individual more than to place responsibility on him, and to let him know that you trust him.
—Booker T. Washington

Men have never been individually self-sufficient.
—Reinhold Niebuhr

Teamwork

The way a team plays as a whole determines its success. You may have the greatest bunch of individual stars in the world, but if they don't play together, the club won't be worth a dime.

—Babe Ruth

We must, indeed, all hang together or, most assuredly, we shall all hang separately.

—Benjamin Franklin

When a gifted team dedicates itself to unselfish trust and combines instinct with boldness and effort, its ready to climb.

—Pat Riley

Quote

Alone we can do so little; together we can do so much.

— Helen Keller

There are no problems we cannot solve together, and very few that we can solve by ourselves.

— Lyndon B. Johnson

One of the best ways to persuade others is with your ears — by listening to them.

— Dean Rusk

I not only use all the brains I have but all I can borrow.

—Woodrow T. Wilson

*I*f a team is to reach its potential, each player must be willing to subordinate his personal goals to the good of the team.

—Bud Wilkinson

*I*t is well known that the era of the rugged individual has been replaced by the era of the team player.

—Margaret Wheatly

Quote

$\mathcal{H}$ere's what is exciting about sharing ideas with others: If you share a new idea with ten people, they get to hear it once and you get to hear it ten times.

—Jim Rohn

$\mathcal{I}$'ll lift you and you lift me, and we'll both ascend together.

—John Greenleaf Whittier

$\mathcal{W}$e must learn to live together as brothers or perish together as fools.

—Martin Luther King, Jr.

Teamwork

*I*t is literally true that you can succeed best and quickest by helping others to succeed.

—Napoleon Hill

*T*he important thing to recognize is that it takes a team, and the team ought to get credit for the wins and the losses. Successes have many fathers, failures have none.

—Philip Caldwell

*N*ever tell people how to do things. Tell them what to do and they will surprise you with their ingenuity.

—George S. Patton

Gettin' good players is easy. Gettin' 'em to play together is the hard part.
— Casey Stengel

Everybody on a championship team doesn't get publicity, but everyone can say he's a champion.
— Earvin "Magic" Johnson

Synergy — the bonus that is achieved when things work together harmoniously.
— Mark Twain

*C*ommunicate, communicate, and then communicate some more.

— Bob Nelson

*D*ependent people need others to get what they want. Independent people can get what they want through their own efforts. Interdependent people combine their own efforts with the efforts of others to achieve their greatest success.

— Stephen R. Covey

*T*he moment we break faith with one another, the sea engulfs us and the light goes out.

— James Baldwin

Quote

No one lives long enough to learn everything they need to learn starting from scratch. To be successful, we absolutely, positively have to find people who have already paid the price to learn the things that we need to learn to achieve our goals.

—Brian Tracy

The welfare of each is bound up in the welfare of all.

—Helen Keller

When building a team, always look for people who love to win. If you can't find any of those, search for people who hate to lose.

—H. Ross Perot

Teamwork

𝒯rust is the lubrication that makes it possible for organizations to work.

—Warren Bennis

𝒯eamwork divides the task and doubles the success.

—Source Unknown

𝒩ever doubt that a small group of thoughtful, committed citizens can change the world. Indeed, it is the only thing that ever has.

—Margaret Mead

Quote

*I*n organizations, real power and energy is generated through relationships. The patterns of relationships and the capacities to form them are more important than tasks, functions, roles, and positions.

— Margaret Wheatly

*W*e cannot be separated in interest or divided in purpose. We stand together until the end.

— Woodrow T. Wilson

*T*o acquire knowledge, one must study; but to acquire wisdom, one must observe.

— Marilyn vos Savant

Individual commitment to a group effort—that is what makes a team work, a company work, a society work, a civilization work.

—Vince Lombardi

None of us is as smart as all of us.
—Ken Blanchard

There can only be one state of mind as you approach any profound test; total concentration, a spirit of togetherness, and strength.

—Pat Riley

Keep away from people who try to belittle your ambitions. Small people do that, but great people make you feel that you, too, can become great.

— Mark Twain

If you wish to win a man over to your ideas, first make him your friend.

— Abraham Lincoln

The best way to inspire people to superior performance is to convince them by everything you do and by your everyday attitude that you are wholeheartedly supporting them.

— Harold S. Geneen

Teamwork

TEAM—Together Everyone Achieves More.

—Source Unknown

When a team outgrows individual performance and learns team confidence, excellence becomes a reality.

—Joe Paterno

The strength of the team is each individual member... the strength of each member is the team.

—Phil Jackson

Surround yourself with people who take their work seriously, but not themselves, those who work hard and play hard.

—Colin Powell

The most important single ingredient in the formula of success is knowing how to get along with people.

—Theodore Roosevelt

Problems can become opportunities when the right people come together.

—Robert Redford

Outstanding leaders go out of their way to boost the self-esteem of their personnel. If people believe in themselves, it's amazing what they can accomplish.

—Sam Walton

Our best thoughts come from others.
—Ralph Waldo Emerson

You can have everything in life you want if you just help enough other people get what they want.

—Zig Ziglar

They may beat us by outplaying us; they may beat us by outcoaching us; but nobody will ever beat us by out-working us.

— Woody Hayes

Talent wins games, but teamwork and intelligence wins championships.

— Michael Jordan

Working together, ordinary people can perform extraordinary feats. They can push things that come into their hands a little higher up, a little further on towards the heights of excellence.

— Source Unknown

Teamwork

If there is any one secret of success, it lies in the ability to get the other person's point of view and see things from that person's angle as well as from your own.

—Henry Ford

Those who trust us educate us.

—T. S. Eliot

The key elements in the art of working together are how to deal with change, how to deal with conflict, and how to reach our potential . . . the needs of the team are best met when we meet the needs of individuals persons.

—Max DePree

A house divided against itself cannot stand.

— Abraham Lincoln

Being a part of success is more important than being personally indispensable.

— Pat Riley

Your ability to communicate is an important tool in your pursuit of your goals, whether it is with your family, your co-workers or your clients and customers.

— Les Brown

Teamwork

*Y*ou can impress people from a distance, but you can only impact them close up.

— Howard Hendricks

*I*n the end, all business operations can be reduced to three words: people, product and profits. Unless you've got a good team, you can't do much with the other two.

— Lee Iacocca

*I*t is amazing how much you can accomplish when it doesn't matter who gets the credit.

— Harry S Truman

My mentor said, "Let's go do it", not "You go do it." How powerful when someone says, "Let's!"

— Jim Rohn

It is not from ourselves that we learn to be better than we are.

— Wendell Berry

People have been known to achieve more as a result of working with others than against them.

— Dr. Allan Fromme

Teamwork

There is great comfort and inspiration in the feeling of close human relationships and its bearing on our mutual fortunes—a powerful force to overcome the "tough breaks" which are certain to come to most of us from time to time.

— Walt Disney

If you have knowledge, let others light their candles with it.

— Margaret Fuller

When your team is winning, be ready to be tough, because winning can make you soft. On the other hand, when your team is losing, stick by them. Keep believing.

— Bo Schembechler

Quote

*Y*ou will find men who want to be carried on the shoulders of others, who think that the world owes them a living. They don't seem to see that we must all lift together and pull together.

—Henry Ford

*P*eople who work together will win, whether it be against complex football defenses, or the problems of modern society.

—Vince Lombardi

*T*o succeed in business it is necessary to make others see things as you see them.

—John H. Patterson

Teamwork

It's the pack that gets the job done, not the lone wolf.

—Mike O'Neil

No matter what accomplishments you make, somebody helped you.

—Althea Gibson

Teamwork means that we share a common ideal, embrace a common goal. regardless of our differences, we strive shoulder to shoulder, confident in one another's faith, trust, and commitment. In the end, teamwork can be summed up in five short words: we believe in each other.

—Source Unknown

Unquote

Unquote

A dream doesn't become reality through magic; it takes sweat, determination and hard work.

— Colin Powell

*T*he achievements of an organization are the results of the combined effort of each individual.

— Vince Lombardi

*D*on't wish it was easier; wish you were better. Don't wish for less problems; wish for more skills. Don't wish for less challenges; wish for more wisdom.

— Jim Rohn

Opportunity lies in the man and not in the job.

—Zig Ziglar

Sweat plus sacrifice equals success.

—Charlie Finley

We lift ourselves by our thought, we climb upon our vision of ourselves. If you want to enlarge your life, you must first enlarge your thought of it and of yourself. Hold the ideal of yourself as you long to be, always, everywhere—your ideal of what you long to attain—the ideal of health, efficiency, success.

—Orison Swett Marden

Unquote

The man who is intent on making the most of his opportunities is too busy to bother about luck.

— B. C. Forbes

The heights by great men reached and kept
Were not attained by sudden flight,
But they, while their companions slept
Were toiling upward in the night.

— Henry Wadsworth Longfellow

We have to do the best we can. This is our sacred human responsibility.

— Albert Einstein

Teamwork

The only honest measure of your success is what you are doing compared to your true potential.

— Paul J. Meyer

Surround yourself with the best people you can find, delegate authority, and don't interfere.

— Ronald Reagan

I come to the office each morning and stay for long hours doing what has to be done to the best of my ability. And when you've done the best you can, you can't do any better.

— Harry S Truman

If you can't do great things, do small things in a great way. Don't wait for great opportunities. Seize common, everyday ones and make them great.

— Napoleon Hill

I know the price of success: dedication, hard work, and a devotion to things you want to see happen.

— Frank Lloyd Wright

You can have anything you want—if you want it badly enough. You can be anything you want to be, have anything you desire, accomplish anything you set out to accomplish—if you will hold to that desire with singleness of purpose.

— Robert Collier

Teamwork

Champions believe in themselves even if no one else does.

—Source Unknown

Act so as to elicit the best in others and thereby in thyself.

—Felix Adler

People become really quite remarkable when they start thinking that they can do things. When they believe in themselves they have the first secret of success.

—Norman Vincent Peale

Do a little more each day than you think you possibly can.

— Lowell Thomas

One machine can do the work of fifty ordinary men. No machine can do the work of one extraordinary man.

— Elbert Hubbard

Nothing great was ever achieved without enthusiasm.

— Ralph Waldo Emerson

Teamwork

When we have begun to take charge of our lives, to own ourselves, there is no longer any need to ask permission of someone.

— George O'Neil

I don't know the key to success, but the key to failure is trying to please everybody.

— Bill Cosby

The mind is the limit. As long as the mind can envision the fact that you can do something, you can do it — as long as you really believe 100%.

— Arnold Schwarzenegger

Duty is the most sublime word in our language. Do your duty in all things. You cannot do more. You should never wish to do less.

—Robert E. Lee

The price of success is hard work, dedication to the job at hand, and the determination that whether we win or lose, we have applied the best of ourselves to the task at hand.

—Vince Lombardi

"I can't do it" never yet accomplished anything; "I will try" has performed wonders.

—George Burnham

Teamwork

I am only one, but still, I am one. I cannot do everything but I can do something. And, because I cannot do everything, I will not refuse to do what I can.

—Edward Everett Hale

I don't compete with other discus throwers. I compete with my own history.

—Al Oerter

*T*he truth is that all of us attain the greatest success and happiness possible in this life whenever we use our native capacities to their greatest extent.

—Smiley Blanton

Nothing will work unless you do.
—John Wooden

Nobody can do it for you.
—Darren Roberts

People who have accomplished work worthwhile have had a very high sense of the way to do things. They have not been content with mediocrity. They have not confined themselves to the beaten tracks; they have never been satisfied to do things just as others do them, but always a little better. They always pushed things that came to their hands a little higher up, a little farther on, and that counts in the quality of life's work. It is constant effort to be first-class in everything one attempts that conquers the heights of excellence.
—Orison Swett Marden

Teamwork

𝒯hose who consciously purpose themselves in doing nothing less than "exceeding the mark," never have to question whether or not they will "meet the mark"!

—Brian G. Jett

𝒩ature arms each man with some faculty which enables him to do easily some feat impossible to any other.

—Ralph Waldo Emerson

𝒥've always tried to do my best on the ball field. I can't do any more than that. I always try to give 100%; and if my team loses, I come back and give 100% the next day.

—Jesse Barfield

*H*old yourself responsible to a higher standard than anybody else expects of you; never excuse yourself.

— Henry Ward Beecher

---

*M*y mother drew a distinction between achievement and success. She said that achievement is the knowledge that you have studied and worked hard and done the best that is in you. Success is being praised by others, and that's nice too, but not as important or satisfying. Always aim for achievement and forget about success.

— Helen Hayes

---

*D*o what you can, with what you have, where you are.

— Theodore Roosevelt

Teamwork

*T*he person who knows one thing and does it better than anyone else, even if it only be the art of raising lentils, receives the crown he merits. If he raises all his energy to that end, he is a benefactor of mankind and is rewarded as such.

—Og Mandino

*I*t is always easier—and usually far more effective—to focus on changing your behavior than on changing the behavior of others.

—Bob Nelson

I know that no one can really stop me but myself and that really no one can help me but myself.

—Peter Nivio Zarlenga

Unquote

The most successful men in the end are those whose success is the result of steady accretion. It is the man who carefully advances step by step, with his mind becoming wider and wider—and progressively better able to grasp any theme or situation—persevering in what he knows to be practical, and concentrating his thought upon it, who is bound to succeed in the greatest degree.

—Alexander Graham Bell

Put the uncommon effort into the common task—make it large by doing it in a great way.

—Orison Swett Marden

Well done is better than well said.

—Benjamin Franklin

Teamwork

Never neglect details. When everyone's mind is dulled or distracted the leader must be doubly vigilant.

— Colin Powell

Success is the person who year after year reaches the highest limits in his field.

— Sparky Anderson

A man can only be reliant on the success he creates himself.

— Paul Oliver

Nothing can stop the man with the right mental attitude from achieving his goal; nothing on earth can help the man with the wrong mental attitude.
— Thomas Jefferson

I have always tried to go a step past wherever people expected me to end up.
— Beverly Sills

It is easy in the world to live after the world's opinion; it is easy in solitude after one's own; but the great man is he who in the midst of the crowd keeps with perfect sweetness the independence of solitude.
— Ralph Waldo Emerson

Teamwork

*W*henever you are asked if you can do a job, tell em, "Certainly I can!"—and get busy and find out how to do it.

—Theodore Roosevelt

---

*G*enius is one percent inspiration and ninety-nine percent perspiration!

—Thomas A. Edison

---

*I*f you want to be creative in your company, your career, your life, all it takes is one easy step . . . the extra one. When you encounter a familiar plan, you just ask one question: What ELSE could we do?

—Dale Dauten

Unquote

Men who have attained things worth having in this world have worked while others idled, have persevered while others gave up in despair, have practiced early in life the valuable habits of self-denial, industry, and singleness of purpose. As a result, they enjoy in later life the success so often erroneously attributed to good luck.

—Grenville Kleiser

The principle is competing against yourself. It's about self improvement, about being better than you were the day before.

—Steve Young

Do something—lead, follow, or get out of the way.

—George S. Patton

Teamwork

𝒯he quality of a person's life is in direct proportion to their commitment to excellence, regardless of their chosen field of endeavor.

—Vince Lombardi

ℐ found that the men and women who got to the top were those who did the jobs they had in hand, with everything they had of energy and enthusiasm and hard work.

—Harry S Truman

𝒯he best job goes to the person who can get it done without passing the buck or coming back with excuses.

—Napoleon Hill

The truth of the matter is that you always know the right thing to do. The hard part is doing it.

— Norman Schwarzkopf

I hope I have convinced you — the only thing that separates successful people from the ones who aren't is the willingness to work very, very hard.

— Helen Gurley Brown

Every job is a self-portrait of the person who does it. Autograph your work with excellence.

— Source Unknown

Teamwork

Those who are fired with an enthusiastic idea and who allow it to take hold and dominate their thoughts find that new worlds open for them. As long as enthusiasm holds out, so will new opportunities.

—Norman Vincent Peale

Whenever you do a thing, act as if all the world were watching.

—Thomas Jefferson

It is an immutable law in business that words are words, explanations are explanations, promises are promises but only performance is reality.

—Harold S. Geneen

Blessed is the man who has some congenial work, some occupation in which he can put his heart, and which affords a complete outlet to all the forces there are in him.

—John Burroughs

Nothing strengthens the judgment and quickens the conscience like individual responsibility.

—Elizabeth Cady Stanton

Average people look for ways of getting away with it; successful people look for ways of getting on with it.

—Jim Rohn

You don't make progress by standing on the sidelines, whimpering and complaining. You make progress by implementing ideas.

— Shirley Chisholm

If I want to be great I have to win the victory over myself . . . self-discipline.

— Harry S Truman

Keep a definite goal of achievement constantly in view. Realize that work well and worthily done makes life truly worth living.

— Grenville Kleiser

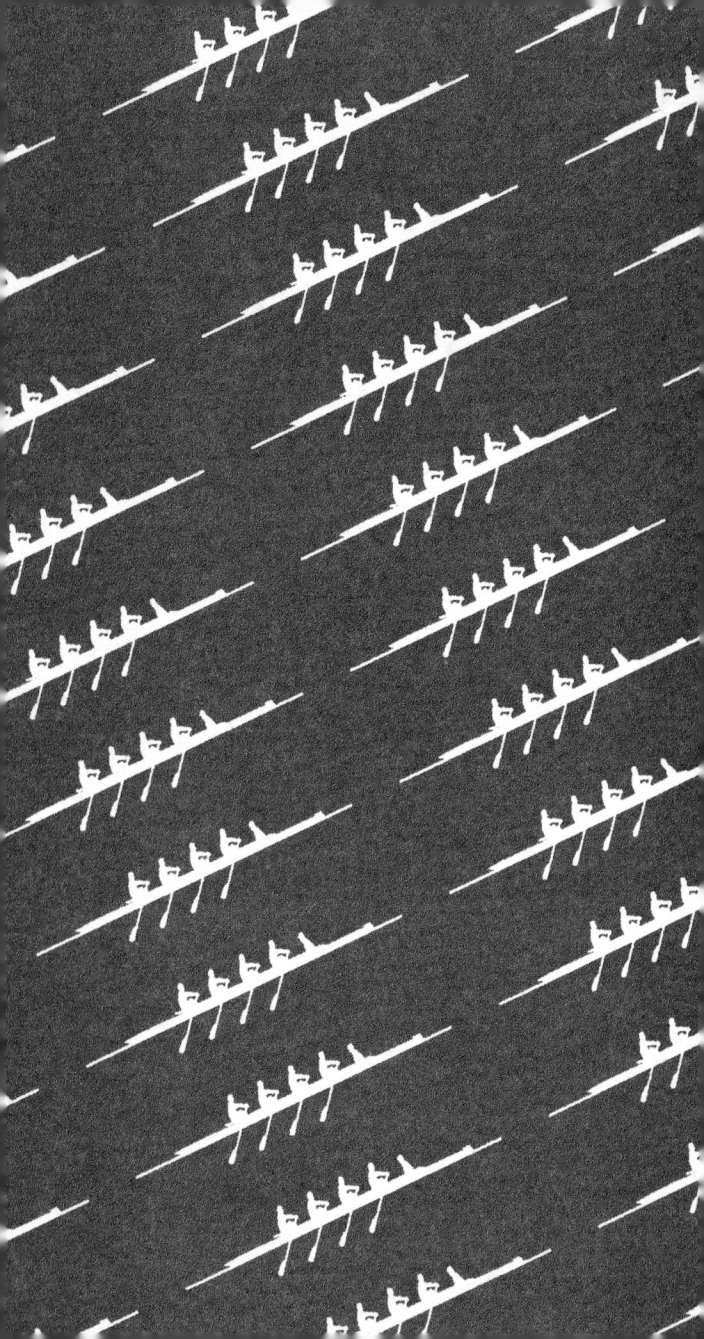